Australia • Brazil • Japan • Korea • Mexico • Singapore • Spain • United Kingdom • United States

Getting the Picture

Fast Forward
Purple Level 20

Text: Carmel Reilly
Editor: Johanna Rohan
Design: James Lowe
Series design: James Lowe
Production controller: Seona Galbally
Photo research: Gillian Cardinal
Audio recordings: Juliet Hill, Picture Start
Spoken by: Matthew King and Abbe Holmes
Reprint: Siew Han Ong

Acknowledgements
The author and publisher would like to acknowledge permission to reproduce material from the following sources: Photographs by Corbis Australia/Michael Freeman, pp 3, 9/ Hulton-Deutsch Collection, p 8 top/ Bettmann, pp 8 bottom, 11/ Royalty-Free, p 14; Fotolia.com/Tom Schmucker, p 19; Getty Images/John Lund, p 15/ John Lawrence, back cover, pp 18 bottom, 23 left/ Burazin, pp 20, 23 right; Istockphoto, p 17 bottom/ Robert Goldberg, p 4 left/ Steve Geer, p 4 right/ Johnny Lye, p 7 bottom; PhotoEdit/David Young-Wolff, p 21 top/ Bill Aron, p 21 bottom; Photolibrary/Yannick, cover bottom righ & left, p 5/ Bill Bachmann, p 13/ Image 100, p 16/ SuperStock, pp 17 top, 18 top; Science & Society Picture Library, cover top, pp 6, 7 top, 9 top, 10, 12, 22.

ISBN 978 0 17 012663 2
ISBN 978 0 17 012657 1 (set)

Cengage Learning Australia
Level 7, 80 Dorcas Street
South Melbourne, Victoria Australia 3205
Phone: 1300 790 853

Cengage Learning New Zealand
Unit 4B Rosedale Office Park
331 Rosedale Road, Albany, North Shore NZ 0632
Phone: 0508 635 766

For learning solutions, visit cengage.com.au

Printed in Australia by Ligare Pty Ltd
6 7 8 9 10 11 12 20 19 18 17 16

THE UNIVERSITY OF
MELBOURNE

Evaluated in independent research by staff from the Department of Language, Literacy and Arts Education at the University of Melbourne.

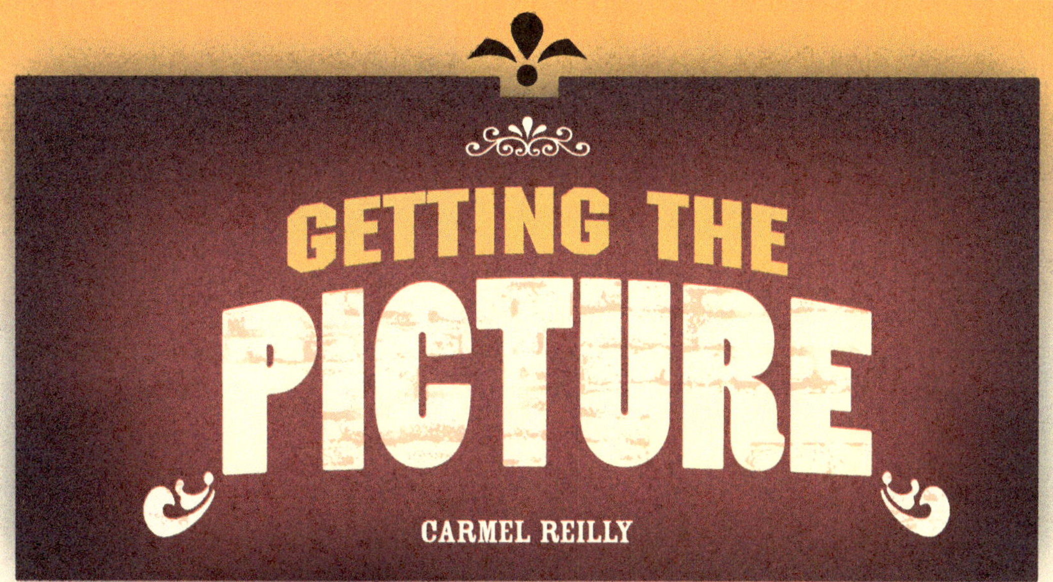

GETTING THE PICTURE

CARMEL REILLY

Contents

Chapter 1

PHOTOGRAPHY

Photography is a way of making pictures by using light.

Photography

The word photography means 'to draw with light'.

It comes from two Greek words – 'photos' meaning light, and 'graphe' meaning to write or draw.

A camera is used to take a photograph.
The camera focuses **reflected** light
from an object, or scene,
and **records** this light onto film
or a **digital chip**.

The film, or information on the digital chip,
can then be **processed** into a photo.

The idea of taking photographs has been around for hundreds of years. However, it wasn't until 1826 that an inventor was able to take the first photograph. He took this photograph by covering a metal plate with **light-sensitive** chemicals and exposing it to light through a camera **lens**.

very early cameras

Over the next 50 years, photographers moved from using metal plates to glass plates and finally to light-sensitive film to record an image.

This camera, from 1925, uses light-sensitive film.

Today, light-sensitive film is still used. However, digital technology has become more popular, and most images are now recorded inside cameras on a digital chip.

a digital camera

Chapter 2

THE FIRST PHOTOGRAPHERS

The first photographers were inventors, scientists and artists.
They built their own cameras, and knew how to use chemicals to process their photos.

Joseph Nicéphore Niépce

The world's first photograph was taken by Joseph Nicéphore Niépce, in 1826.

It wasn't easy to use these early cameras.

It could take more than a minute to take a photograph and the plates had to be processed straightaway so that the image wouldn't be lost.

Chapter 3

USING FILM

By the 1880s,
photographers started to use film
instead of plates in cameras.

This made taking photos easier
because many shots could be taken
on one roll of film.

Cameras became smaller
because film was small and light
and took up less space inside the cameras
than the plates.

Also, by the 1880s,
cameras started to be sold
to the public.
These cameras were smaller,
cheaper and easier to use than
the early cameras.

As a result,
many people took up photography
as a hobby.

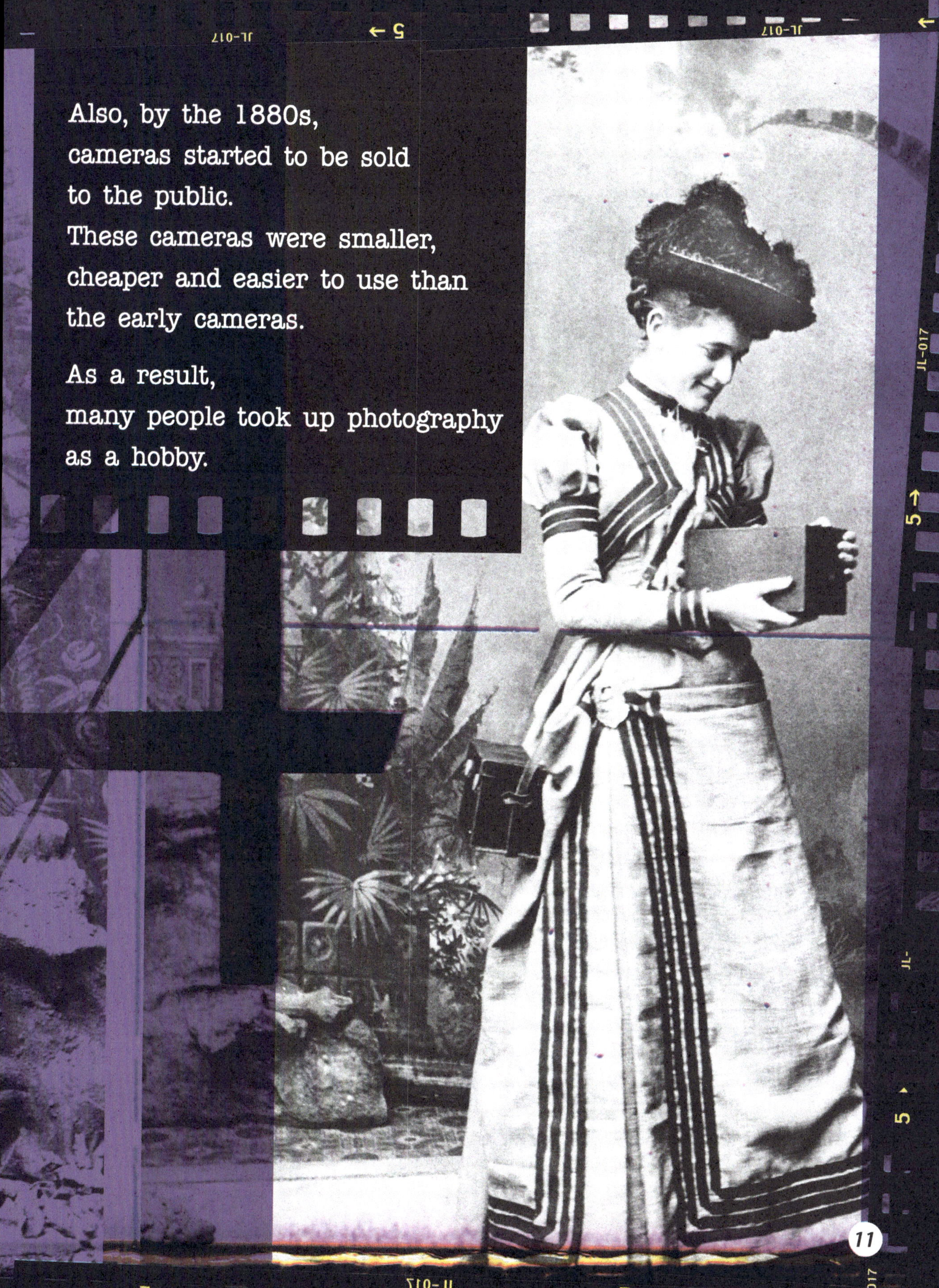

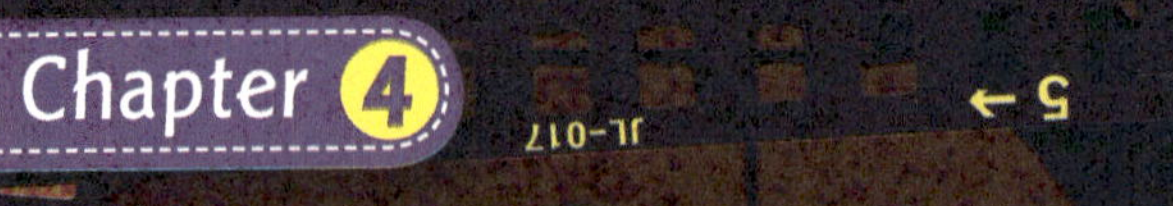

Chapter 4

FILM PHOTOGRAPHY

In the 1900s,
more people started taking photos,
but few of them processed
their own film.
This was because it was expensive
to buy the equipment and chemicals needed.
It was also expensive to set up a darkroom.

processing film in a darkroom

However, some people did process their own film and today there are still photographers who like to take photos on film and process it themselves.

How to Process Film

Process film in a darkroom
in the following way:

1. Place the film in a chemical solution to make the image appear.
2. Place the film in another chemical solution to 'fix' the image.
3. Put the film in the enlarger with the light-sensitive photographic paper below it.

4. Shine the light through the film and onto the paper.
5. Put the paper in another chemical solution to make the image appear as a photograph.

Chapter 5

DIGITAL PHOTOGRAPHY

Digital cameras were first used at the end of the 20th century.

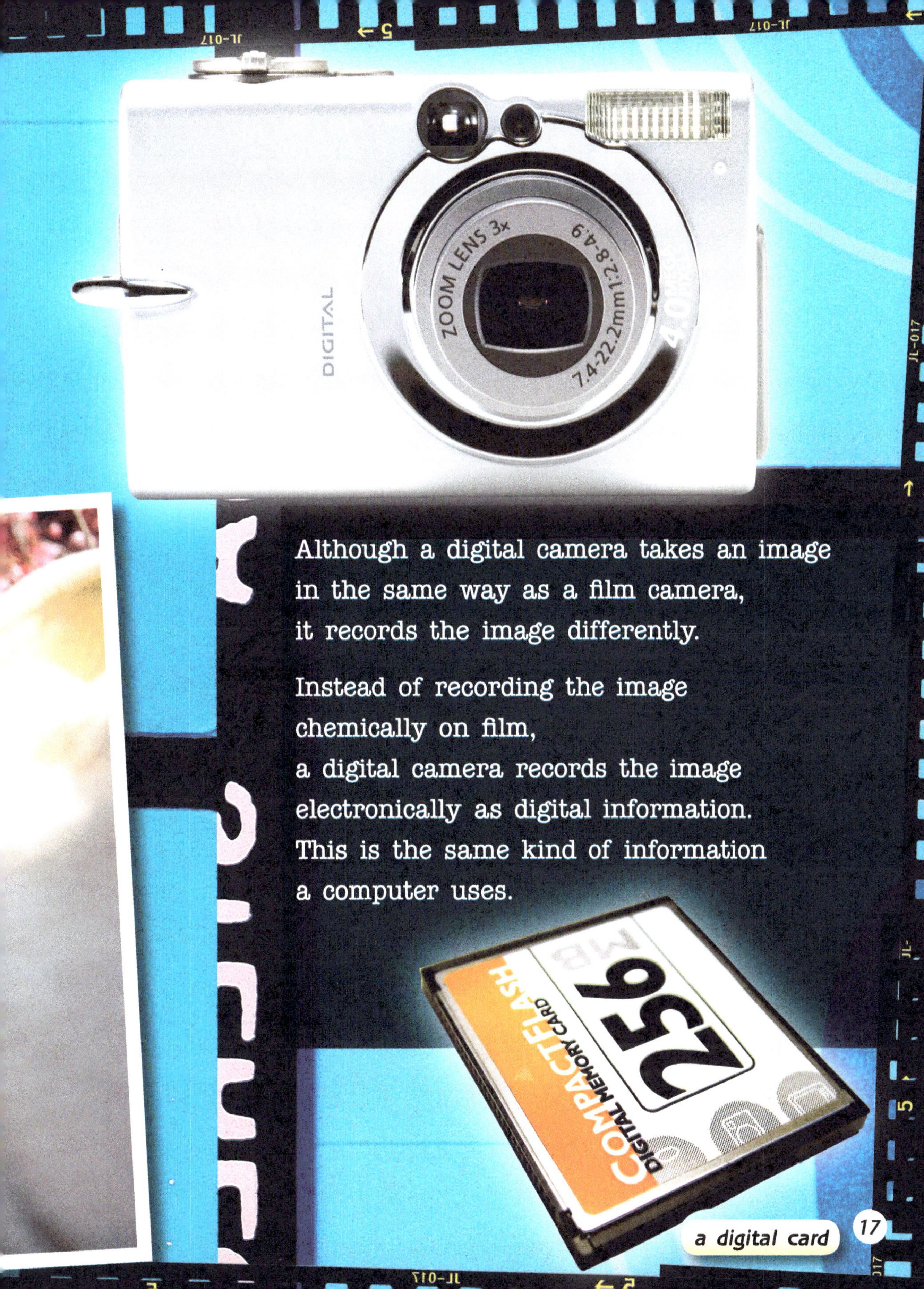

Although a digital camera takes an image in the same way as a film camera, it records the image differently.

Instead of recording the image chemically on film, a digital camera records the image electronically as digital information. This is the same kind of information a computer uses.

a digital card

Digital cameras became popular very quickly. Most people take photos with them rather than with film cameras.

People like to use digital cameras for a number of reasons:

- they are small and easy to use
- they have screens that let the photographer see the picture straightaway

- if the image is not right, it can be deleted from the camera
- the image can be changed later with a computer program.

How to Process Digital Photos

Anyone with a computer and printer
can process their digital photos in the following way:

1. Move the photographic files from the camera onto a special photographic program on the computer.

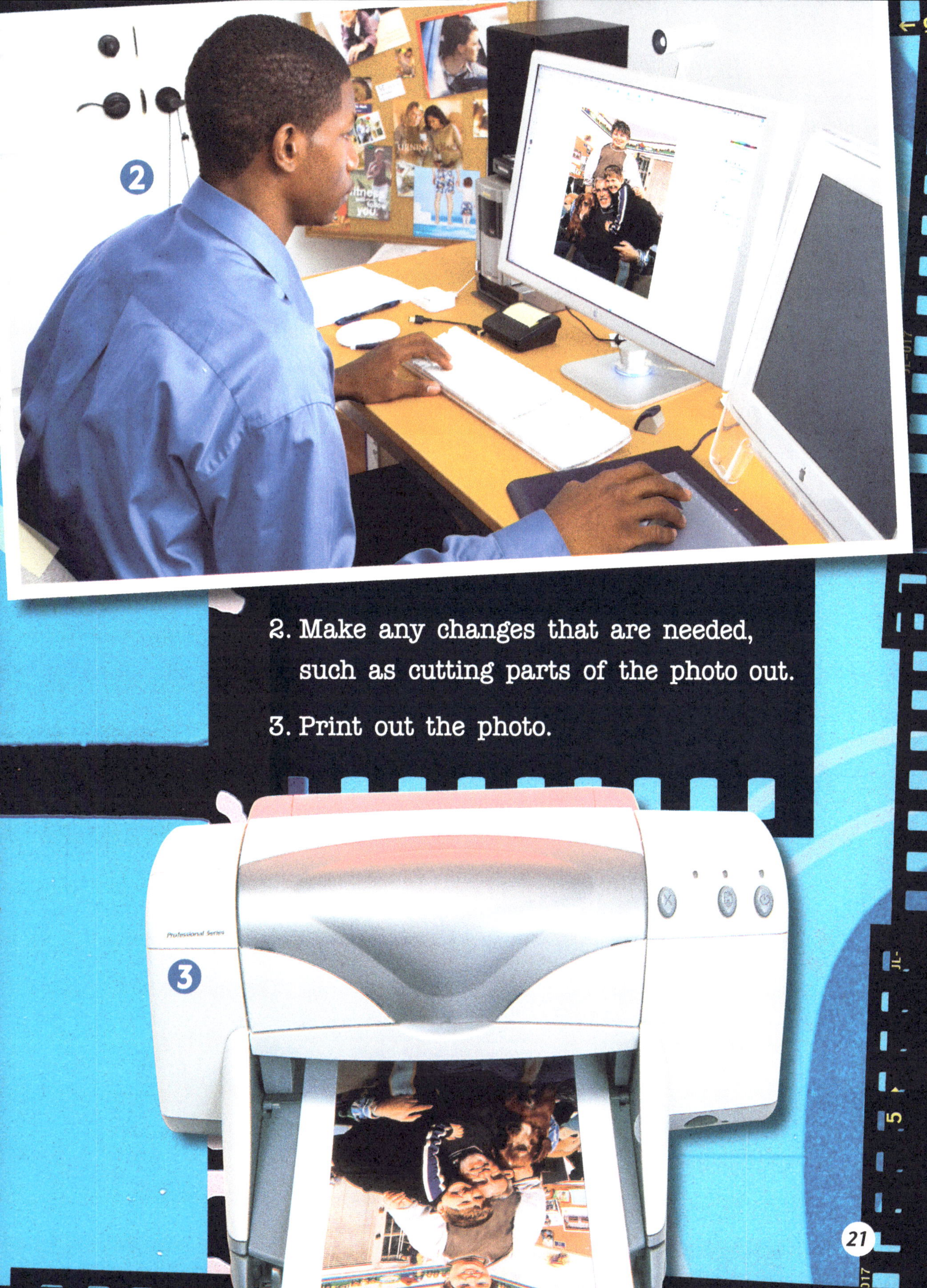

2. Make any changes that are needed, such as cutting parts of the photo out.

3. Print out the photo.

Chapter 6

SUMMARY

When photography first began,
very few people were able to use cameras.
They were large and expensive.
Only photographers knew how to use them
and how to process the plates or film.

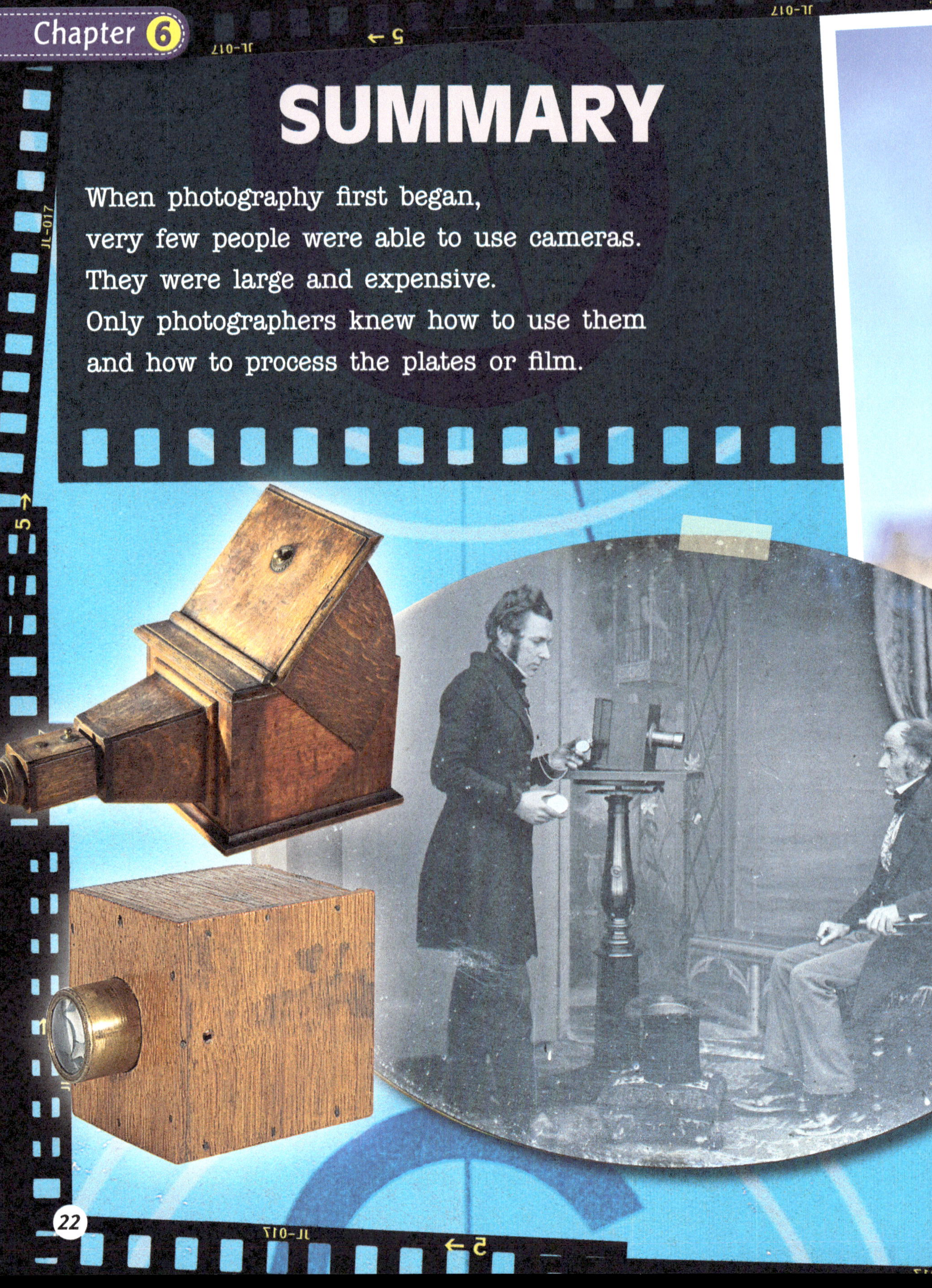

Today, cameras are small and quite cheap. They are easy to use and can be connected to a computer program that can make changes to the image and print out the photo.

These days, it's easy for anyone to take and to process photos.

Glossary

digital chip a small electronic device that can store information

lens the part of a camera that focuses the image

light-sensitive something that reacts in a certain way when exposed to light

processed changed into a form that can be easily viewed

records preserves in a permanent form

reflected light that has bounced off something else

Index